ARCHITECTURE OF INDIA 2.0 (B&W)

I0483039

MR VIVEK KUMAR PANDEY
SHAMBHUNATH

Contents

CHAPTER ONE

Monument

The Monument to Nicholas Ifrom Saint Isaac's Squarein Saint Petersburg(Russia)

The Great Pyramidof Gizabuilt almost 5000 years ago as pharaoh's tomb, one of the Seven Wondersand enduring symbol of ancient Egyptian civilizationsince antiquity.

The Parthenonis regarded as an enduring symbol of Ancient Greece, the Athenian democracy, as well as the symbol of Western Civilization.

The ColosseumFlavian amphitheatre in Rome, a popular monument of the Roman Empire.

The Great Wall of China, a massive fortification structure that became the monument of Chinese civilization.

The Dome of the Rock, a shrine on the Temple Mountin the Old City of Jerusalem, covering the Foundation Stonewhich bears great significance for Muslims, Christians and Jews.

The Christ the King, in Almada, Portugal, has become one of the most visited national monuments.

The Taj Mahalin Agra, one of the most well known National Monuments in India

Amonumentis a type of structurethat was explicitly created to commemorate a person or event, or which has become relevant to a social group as a part of their remembrance of historic times or cultural heritage, due to its artistic, historical, political, technical or architectural importance. Some of the first monuments were dolmens or menhirs, megalithic constructions built for religious or funerary purposes.[1]Examples of monuments include statues, (war) memorials, historical buildings, archaeological sites, and cultural assets. If there is a public interest in its preservation, a monument can for example be listed as a UNESCO World Heritage Site.[2]

Contents

Etymology

The origin of the word "monument" comes from the Greek *mnemosynon* and the Latin *moneo*, *monere*, which means 'to remind', 'to advise' or 'to warn',[3]suggesting a monument allows us to see the past thus helping us visualize what is to come in the future.[4]In Englishthe word "monumental" is often used in reference to something of extraordinary size and power, as in monumental sculpture, but also to mean simply anything made to commemorate the dead, as a funerary monumentor other example of funerary art.

Creation and functions

Monuments have been created for thousands of years, and they are often the most durable and famous symbols of ancient civilizations. Prehistoric tumuli, dolmens, and similar structures have been created in a large number of prehistoric cultures across the world, and the many forms of monumental tombs of the more wealthy and powerful members of a society are often the source of much of our information and art from those cultures.[5]As societies became organized on a larger scale, so monuments so large as to be difficult to destroy like the EgyptianPyramids, the GreekParthenon, the Great Wall of China, IndianTaj Mahalor the Moaiof Easter Islandhave become symbols of their civilizations. In more recent times, monumental structures such as the Statue of Libertyand Eiffel Towerhave become iconic emblems of modern nation-states. The term *monumentality* relates to the symbolic status and physical presence of a monument. In this context, German art historian Helmut Scharf states that "A monument exists in the form of an object and also as symbol thereof. As a language symbol, a monument usually refers to something concrete, in some rare cases it is also used metaphorically .... A monument can be a language symbol for a unity of several monuments ... or only for a single one, but in a broader sense it can also be used in nearly all knowable planes of being. ... What is considered a monument always depends on the importance it attributes to the prevailing or traditional consciousness of a specific historical and social situation."

Basically, the definition framework of the term monument depends on the current historical frame conditions. Aspects of the Culture of Remembrance and cultural memory are also linked to it, as well as questions about the concepts of public sphere and durability (of the one memorized) and the form and content of the monument (work-like monument). From an art historical point of view, the dichotomy of content and form opens up the problem of the "linguistic ability" of the monument. It becomes clear that language is an eminent part of a monument and it is often represented in "non-objective" or "architectural monuments", at least with a plaque. In this connection, the debate touches on the social mechanisms that combine with Remembrance. These are acceptance of the monument as an object, the conveyed contents and the impact of these contents.

Monuments are frequently used to improve the appearance of a city or location. Planned cities such as Washington D.C., New Delhiand Brasíliaare often built around monuments. For example, the Washington Monument's location was conceived by L'Enfantto help organize public space in the city, before it was designed or constructed. Older cities have monuments placed at locations that are already important or are sometimes redesigned to focus on one. As Shelleysuggested in his famous poem "Ozymandias" (*Look on my works, ye Mighty, and despair!*"), the purpose of monuments is very often to impress or awe.

Structures created for others purposes that have been made notable by their age, size or historic significance may also be regarded as monuments. This can happen because of great age and size, as in the case of the Great Wall of China, or because an event of great importance occurred there such as the village of Oradour-sur-Glanein France. Many countries use Ancient monumentor similar terms for the official designation of protected structures or archeological siteswhich may originally have been ordinary domestic houses or other buildings.

Monuments are also often designed to convey historical or political information, and they can thus develop an active socio-political potency. They can be used to reinforce the primacy of contemporary political power, such as the column of Trajanor the numerous statues of Leninin the Soviet Union. They can be used to educate the populace about important events or figures from the past, such as in the renaming of the old General Post Office Building in New York City to the James A. Farley Building (James Farley Post Office), after former Postmaster General James Farley.[6]To fulfill its informative and educative functions a monument needs to be open to the public, which means that its spatial dimension as well as its content can be experienced by the public, and be sustainable. The former may be achieved either by situating the monument in public space or by a public discussion about the monument and its meaning, the latter by the materiality of the monument or if its content immediately becomes part of the collective or cultural memory.

The social meanings of monuments are rarely fixed and certain and are frequently 'contested' by different social groups. As an example: whilst the former East German socialist state may have seen the Berlin Wall as a means of 'protection' from the ideological impurity of the west, dissidents and others would often argue that it was symbolic of the inherent repression and paranoia of that state. This contention of meaning is a central theme of modern 'post processual' archaeological discourse.

Protection and preservation

The term is often used to describe any structure that is a significant and legally protected historic work, and many countries have equivalents of what is called in United

Kingdomlegislation a Scheduled Monument, which often include relatively recent buildings constructed for residential or industrial purposes, with no thought at the time that they would come to be regarded as "monuments".

Until recently, it was customary for archaeologiststo study large monuments and pay less attention to the everyday lives of the societies that created them. New ideas about what constitutes the archaeological recordhave revealed that certain legislative and theoretical approaches to the subject are too focused on earlier definitions of monuments. An example has been the United Kingdom's Scheduled Ancient Monumentlaws.

Other than municipal or national government that protecting the monuments in their jurisdiction, there are institutions dedicated on the efforts to protect and preserve monuments that considered to possess special natural or cultural significance for the world, such as UNESCO's World Heritage Siteprogramme[7]and World Monuments Fund.[2]

Cultural monuments are also considered to be the memory of a community and are therefore particularly at risk in the context of modern asymmetrical warfare. The enemy's cultural heritage is to be sustainably damaged or even destroyed. In addition to the national protection of cultural monuments, international organizations (cf. UNESCO World Heritage, Blue Shield International) therefore try to protect cultural monuments.[8][9][10][11]

Recently, more and more monuments are being preserved digitally (in 3D models) through organisations as CyArk.[12]

Types

Benchmarksplaced by a government agency or private survey firm.

- Buildingsdesigned as landmarks, usually built with an extraordinary feature, such being designed as the tallest, largest, or most distinctive design, e.g., the Burj Khalifain Dubai, the world's tallest structure or the One World Trade Center, the tallest building in the United States, built to memorialize the attack on September 11.
- Cenotaphs(intended to honor the dead who are buried elsewhere) and other memorialsto commemorate the dead, usually war casualties, e.g., India Gateand Vimy Ridge Memorial, or disaster casualties, such as the *Titanic* Memorial, Belfast.
- Church monumentsto commemorate the faithful dead, located above or near their grave, often featuring an effigy, e.g., St. Peter's Basilicaor the medieval church Sta Maria di Collemaggioin L'Aquila.
- Columns, often topped with a statue, e.g., Berlin Victory Column, Nelson's Columnin London, and Trajan's Columnin Rome.
- Eternal flamesthat are kept burning continuously, usually lit to honor unknown soldiers, e.g., at the Tomb of Unknown Soldierin Moscow or at the John F. Kennedy gravesitein Virginia's Arlington National Cemetery.
- Fountains, water-pouring structures usually placed in formal gardensor town squares, e.g., Fontaines de la Concordeand Gardens of Versailles.
- Gravestones, small monuments to the deceased, placed at their gravesites, e.g., the tombs and vaults of veterans in Les Invalidesand Srebrenica Genocide Memorial.
- Mausoleumsand tombsto honor the dead, e.g., the Great Pyramid of Giza, Libyco-Punic Mausoleum of Douggaand Taj Mahal.

- Monoliths erected for religious or commemorative purposes, e.g., Stonehenge.
- Mosque Monuments, places of worship that generally have domes and minarets that stand out against the skyline. They also usually feature highly skilled Islamic calligraphy and geometric artwork, e.g., the Mosque of the Prophet.
- Mounds erected to commemorate great leaders or events, e.g., Kościuszko Mound.
- Obelisks, usually erected to commemorate great leaders, e.g., Cleopatra's Needle in London, the National Monument ("Monas") in Central Jakarta, and the Washington Monument in Washington, D.C.
- Palaces, imposing royal residences designed to impress people with their grandeur and greatness, e.g., Forbidden City in Beijing, Palace of Versailles, and Schwerin Palace in Schwerin.
- Searchlights to project a powerful beam of light, e.g., *Tribute in Light* in the National September 11 Memorial & Museum in New York City, commemorating the September 11 attacks of 2001.
- Statues of famous individuals or symbols, e.g., the Niederwalddenkmal (*Germania*) in Hesse, *Liberty Enlightening the World* (commonly known as the Statue of Liberty) in New York City, and *The Motherland Calls* in Volgograd.
- Temples or religious structures built for pilgrimage, ritual or commemorative purposes, e.g., Borobudur in Magelang and Kaaba in Mecca.
- Terminating vistas, layout design for urban monuments on the end of an avenue, e.g., Opera Garnier in Paris.

- Triumphal arches, almost always to commemorate military successes, e.g., the Arch of Constantine in Rome and Arc de Triomphe de l'Étoile in Paris.
- War memorials, e.g., the Iwo Jima Memorial in Arlington, VA, the Laboe Naval Memorial, the Lorraine American Cemetery and Memorial in St Avold,[13] and the Soviet War Memorial in Berlin.

Architecture of Rajasthan

Jaisalmer Fort, originally including the whole city, dominating the more recent city sections below.

One of the Sahastra Bahu Temples built during the 10th century CE.

The architecture of the Indian state of Rajasthan has usually been a regional variant of the style of Indian architecture prevailing in north India at the time. Rajasthan is especially notable for the forts and palaces of the many Rajput rulers, which are popular tourist attractions.

Most of the population of Rajasthan is Hindu, and there has historically been a considerable Jain minority; this mixture is reflected in the many temples of the region. Māru-Gurjara architecture, or "Solaṅkī style" is a distinctive style that began in Rajasthan and neighbouring Gujarat around the 11th century, and has been revived and taken to other parts of India and the world by both Hindus and Jains. This represents the main contribution of the region to Hindu temple architecture. The Dilwara Jain Temples of Mount Abu built between the 11th and 13th centuries CE are the best-known examples of the style.

Screen of the Adhai Din Ka Jhonpra mosque in Ajmer, by 1199

City Palaceat Jaipurwas designed by Vidyadhar Bhattarcharyaand built between 1729 and 1732. The architecture of the palace shows clear Mughalinfluences on its Rajput Architecture.

The Adhai Din Ka Jhonpramosque in Ajmer(no longer in religious use) is an important early example of Indo-Islamic architecturein a state not otherwise notable for this; though the Ajmer Sharif Dargahis another early building. However there is considerable influence from Mughal architecturein palaces and houses, and Rajasthan has some claim to have sent influence back in elements like the *jharokha* enclosed balcony and *chhatri* open pavilions.

Contents

Common features

The generally arid climate has made stepwells(*baoli* or *bawdi*) more common than in other parts of India, as well as the distinctive covered *taanka* undergroud tanks.

Stone carved *jali*screens are very common, both in temples and secular buildings. As well as palaces, many cities have surviving large townhouses or *haveli* from the last few centuries.

Forts and palaces

Some of the Ahar Cenotaphsoutside Udaipur

See also: List of palaces in Rajasthan

The Hill Forts of Rajasthan(Amer, Chittor, Gagron, Jaisalmer, Kumbhalgarh, Ranthambore), a group of six forts built by various Rajputkingdoms and principalities during the medieval period are among the best examples of Rajput Architecture. The ensemble is also a UNESCO World Heritage Site. Other forts include the Mehrangarh Fortand Jaigarh Fort.

The walledcity of Jaipurwas formed in 1727 by Jai Singh II, and is "a unique example of traditional Hindu town planning",[1]following the precepts set out in much older Hindu texts. Subsequently, the City Palace, Hawa Mahal, Rambagh Palace, Jal Mahaland Albert Hall Museumwere also built. Udaipuralso has several palaces, including the Bagore-ki-Haveli, now a museum, built by an 18th-century chief minister.

The rulers of the princely statesof Rajasthan continued the tradition of building elaborate palaces almost until independence, with examples such as the Lalgarh Palacein Bikaner, Monsoon Palacein Udaipur, and Umaid Bhawan Palacein Jodhpur. Many of these are in versions of Indo-Saracenic architecture, often using European architects.

Cenotaphs

A number of the Rajput dynasties built groups of cenotaphmemorials for their members, mostly using the chatriform, and often at the traditional site for cremations. These include the Ahar Cenotaphsoutside Udaipur, and Bada Baghnear Jaisalmer. Individual examples include the Jaswant Thadaat Jodhpur, and Chaurasi Khambon ki Chhatri, Bundi; there are many others.

History

Ancient

Rajasthan has significant sites of the Bronze AgeIndus Valley Civilization, in particular at Kalibanganand Sothi. The ruined Bairat Stupais the state's main Mauryanand Buddhist site, and appears to have been exceptional at this date, as a large circular shrine or temple around a small stupa.[2]

Hindu temples

Notable early Hindu temples include the early 9th-century Harshat Mata Templeat Abhaneri, where there is also an early stepwell, the Chand Baori, the earliest parts of which are of similar date.[3]The Harshnath Templein Sikar Districtis from around 973, according to an inscription.[4]The Badoli or Baroli Templesare an important group of nine 10th-century Hindu temples in the south-east of the state, no longer in religious use, and with much of the sculpture now in museums, especially the one at Kota.[5]Another group is the two late 10th-century Sahastra Bahu Templesat Nagda.[6]

The small but richly-carved Hindu Ambika Mata templein Jagat, built before 960, is an example of the previous Pratiharastyle transitioning into Māru-Gurjara architecture.[7]On the exteriors, this style is distinguished from other north Indian temple styles of the period in "that the external walls of the temples have been structured by increasing numbers of projections and recesses, accommodating sharply carved statues in niches. These are normally positioned in superimposed registers, above the lower bands of moldings. The latter display continuous lines of horse riders, elephants, and kīrttimukhas. Hardly any segment of the surface is left unadorned." The main shikharatower usually has many *urushringa* subsidiary spirelets on it, and two smaller side-entrances with porches are common in larger temples.[8]

Mandapa ceiling in the Ranakpur Jain Temple

Interiors are if anything even more lavishly decorated, with elaborate carving on most surfaces. In particular, Jain temples often have small low domes carved on the inside with a highly intricate rosette design. Another distinctive feature is "flying" arch-like elements between pillars, touching the horizontal beam above in the centre, and elaborately carved. These have no structural function, and are purely decorative. The style developed large pillared halls, many open at the sides, with Jain temples often having one closed and two pillared halls in sequence on the main axis leading to the shrine.[9]

The style mostly fell from use in Hindu temples in its original regions of Rajasthan and Gujarat by the 13th century, especially as the area had fallen to the Muslim Delhi Sultanateby 1298. But, unusually for an Indian temple style, it continued to be used by Jains there and elsewhere, with a notable "revival" in the 15th century.[10]

The five Kiradu temples, of the 11th or 12th centuries, are examples.[11]The Jagdish Temple, Udaipur(completed 1651) is an example of a Hindu temple using the Māru-Gurjara style at a late date; in this case a commission of

Jagat Singh I, ruler of Mewar.[12]

Jain temples

Significant older Jain temples, or groups of temples, include the Dilwara templeson Mount Abu, the Ranakpur Jain temple,[13]the group at Osian, Jodhpur, including the Mahavira Jain temple, Osian(also early Hindu temples),[14]Mirpur Jain Temple(in fact one of four there), the disputed temple at Rishabhdeo, and the Suswani Matajitemple at Morkhana.

The Kirti Stambhaat Chittor Fortis a spectacular 12th-century tower, carved in Māru-Gurjara style, erected by a Jain merchant.

TOP 10 HISTORICAL MONUMENTS OF INDIA

Description: Mysore Palace

HISTORICAL MONUMENTS
1. HAWA MAHAL

Description: Hawa Mahal

Hawa Mahal stands upright as the entrance to the City Palace, Jaipur. An important landmark in the city, Hawa Mahal is an epitome of the Rajputana architecture. The splendid five-storey "Palace of the Winds" is a blend of beauty and splendor much close to Rajasthan's culture. Maharaja Sawai Pratap Singh built Hawa Mahal in 1779. The pyramid shape of this ancient monument is a tourist attraction having 953 small windows.

2. TAJ MAHAL

Description: Taj mahal

Taj Mahal, the pinnacle of Mughal architecture, was built by the Mughal emperor Shah Jahan (1628-1658), grandson of Akbar the great, in the memory of his queen Arjumand Bano Begum, entitled 'Mumtaz Mahal'. Mumtaz Mahal was a niece of empress Nur Jahan and granddaughter of Mirza Ghias Beg I'timad-ud-Daula, wazir of emperor Jehangir. She was born in 1593 and died in 1631, during the birth of her fourteenth child at Burhanpur. Her mortal remains were temporarily buried in the Zainabad garden. Six months later, her body was transferred to Agra to be finally enshrined in the crypt of the main tomb of the Taj Mahal. The Taj Mahal is the mausoleum of both Mumtaz Mahal and Shah Jahan.

3. MYSORE PALACE

Description: Mysore Palace

The Mysore Palace, Karnataka is popularly known as the the Maharajah's Palace, situated at the city center at Mirza Road. Mysore Palace is one of the most fascinating monument of Mysore city. The other name of the Mysore Palace is Amba Vilas and is the largest palaces of India. Mysore's Wodeyar Mahararajas resided in the Mysore Palace of Karnataka.

The Mysore Palace is a three storied edifice with a length of 245 feet and breadth of 156 feet. The Mysore Palace at Karnataka comprises of a sequence of arched square towers enclosed by domes. The original palace of Mysore was carved out of wood which was accidentally burnt in 1897. The 24th Wodeyar Raja rebuilt the Mysore Palace of Karnataka in 1912. The Mysore Palace followed the Indo-Saracenic style of architecture.

4. VICTORIA MEMORIAL

Description: Victoria Memorial

Victoria Memorial, one of India's most beautiful monuments, represent a unique combination of classical European architecture and Mughal motifs. The domed and white marble museum sprawls over 64 acres and is set in a landscaped garden at the southern side of the Kolkata's maidan (ground) near Jawaharlal Nehru Road.

5. CHARMINAR

Description: Charminar

The charminar Hyderabad's best known landmark was built 1591 by Sultan Mohammed Quli Qutub Shah to appease the force of evil savaging his new city with epidemic and plague. Standing in the heart of the old walled city and surround by lively bazaars, the charminar ('four tower') is a 56m high triumphal arch. The arch is notable for its elegant balconies, stucco decorations and the small mosque, Hyderabad's oldest, on the 2nd floor. An image of the grace every packet of charminar cigarettes, one of India's most popular brand.

6. SANCHI STUPA

Description: Sanchi Stupa

Sanchi is situated in the state of Madhya Pradesh in India. It lies at a distance of approximately 52 km from the capital city of Bhopal and 10 km from Vidisha. The major attractions of Sanchi include a number of Buddhist stupas, monasteries, temples and pillars. All these structures date back to somewhere between 3rd century BC and 12th century AD. The Mauryan emperor Ashoka founded all the stupas at Sanchi in the honor of Lord Buddha. They have the distinction of being included by UNESCO in its list of World Heritage Sites.

7. QUTAB MINAR

Description: Qutab Minar

Qutub-ud-din Aibak laid the foundation for Qutub Minar in 1199 AD and his successor and son-in-law Shamsu'd-Din-Iitutmish completed the structure by adding three more stories. Standing at 72.5 meters, it is the highest stone tower in India. Its base diameter is 14.3 meters and its top diameter is 2.7 meters. It has 379 steps leading to its top story. The lower three stories are made using red sand stone and the top two with marble and sand stone.

8. CELLULAR JAIL

Description: Cellular Jail

The Cellular Jail, also known as Kālā Pānī (Hindi: काला पानी कैद ख़ाना, literally 'black water', in the sense of deep sea and hence exile), was a colonial prison situated in the Andaman and Nicobar Islands, India. The prison was used by the British especially to exile political prisoners to the remote archipelago. Many notable freedom fighters such as Batukeshwar Dutt and Veer Savarkar, among others, were imprisoned here during the struggle for India's independence. Today, the complex serves as a national memorial monument.

9. GATEWAY

Description: Gateway

The majestic Gateway of India is a glorious historical memorial built during British rule. This magnificent monument has been built in Indo-Sarcenic style to commemorate the visit of King George V and Queen Mary to Bombay. Gateway of India is one of the finest example of colonial architectural heritage in India. This grand structure stands at the Apollo Bunder, a popular meeting place in Mumbai. The gateway of India was designed by the British architect George Wittet and was opened for general public in the year 1924.

10. VIDHAN SOUDHA

Description: Vidhan-Soudha

Vidhan Soudha counts amongst the most impressive as well as the most magnificent buildings in the Bangalore city of India. It is mainly famous for housing the Legislative Chambers of the state government. The three hundred rooms of Vidhan Soudha accommodate approximately twenty-two departments of the state government. The building rises to a height of almost 46 m, making it one of the most imposing structures in the city of Bangalore.

Built in the year 1956, Vidhan Soudha of Bangalore boasts of exquisite Dravidian architecture. It was built under the then chief minister of Karnataka, Mr. Kengal Hanumanthaiah, as a tribute to Indian temple architecture. The chief engineer of Vidhan Soudha, B.R. Manickam mainly made use of granite to get the edifice constructed. In the following lines, we have provided more information on the architecture of the Vidhan Soudha of Bangalore, India.

5 Monuments and temples with the best architecture in South India

South India has some of the best monuments and temples that are architecturally brilliant. Some of these historical monuments and temples are visited both by national as well as international tourists. In South India, the temples that were constructed long back can even be classified as monuments because of their old world charm and their architectural profoundness. Let's find out the best temples and monuments that you just need to visit when you have south India on your travel agenda.

Mamallapuram Shore Temple, Chennai

Located in the Kanchipuram district, it is about 60 kms from Chennai. Being one of the oldest temples of the country and a UNESCO World Heritage site, it is also a good example of structural temples made in stone. It was in fact the first building of its time that was made of granite stone rather than rocks. It was built in the 7th century; this temple is a group of three temples located overlooking the Bay of Bengal in Mamallapuram. The temple is literally located on the shore, and an early morning sunrise when the sun shines through the sea onto Shiva Linga in the main shrine is a sight to behold.

Description: 1

Mysore Palace, Mysore

This palace belongs to the royal family of Wodeyar Maharajas. The palace you now see was redesigned and remade by an English architect in 1912. This breathtaking beautiful building has beautiful interiors and you can see different artifacts and paintings inside. One day of the week, the palace is lit with around 10000 light bulbs that make its majestic charm visible.

Description: 2

Meenakshi Temple, Madurai

Meenakshi temple is the temple of Parvati who is the consort of Shiva. It is also one of the few popular temples celebrating a goddess. What makes the temple so epic is the fact that it has 33000 sculptures and is the largest temple complex in the state of Tamil Nadu. The other highlight of the temple is the 14 differently made Gopurams and the thousand pillar hall that has almost 1000 pillars arranged in a fashion that they appear to be in neat rows and columns, no matter which angle you look at them from.Gopurams are pyramid shaped towers that appear mostly in the entrance of temples. It is, in fact a prominent feature of Dravidian architecture.

Description: 3

- <u>wikipedia.org</u>**Charminar, Hyderabad**

Charminar is a famous mosque in the heart of Hyderabad. This place is often recommended to be the top 10 places that need to be on your travel list in India. Built in 1591 by the fifth ruler of the Qualb Shahi dynasty, it is a tourist spot that represents Islamic architecture well. Though the reason why he built it is debated, this monument is famous because of its ornate and beautiful designs. It is during winter that most people visit the mosque. It is a square structure with 20 meters each side and with four arches that face a direction that also opens into four streets. Though it is a piece of Islamic architecture, its architecture is also inspired by Hindu architecture. Many people say that the building does justice to the Hindu and Islamic cultures led by the society of Hyderabad.

Description: 4

Brihadeeshwarar temple, Thanjavur

Built only out of granite, this temple is one of the greatest buildings of the Chola dynasty. Located in the city of Thanjavur, it is a temple dedicated to Lord Brihadeeshwara who was an avatar (form) of Lord Shiva. The most beautiful view is the one inside the temple of Lord Shiva which is one of the biggest idols of the deity. Many say it is one of the temples that showcase Dravidian architecture brilliantly. The temple is also famous for its sculptures of various gods like Dakshinamurthi, Ganesha, Vishnu as well as "Ashta-dikpaalakas" (deities who rule the specific directions of the space) – Indra, Agni, Yama, Nirrti, Varuna, Vayu, Kubera and Isana.

Description: 5

Description: 6

Shop For This Thanjavur Temple at http://tnpoompuhar.org/tamil-nadu/pithwork/thanjavur-temple.html

This entry was posted in History, Thanjavurand tagged Thanjavur, Brihadeeshwarar temple, Hyderabad, Charminar, Madurai, Meenakshi Temple, Mysore, Mysore Palace, Shore Temple, Mamallapuram Shore Temple, architecture in South

India, _the best architecture in South India_, _the best architecture_, _Monuments and temples_, _Monuments and temples with the best architecture in South India_, _5 Monuments and temples with the best architecture in South India_, _Chennai_on February 27, 2015 by Poompuhar.